CAT NIPS!

feline cuisine

& Martha Reynolds

Illustrations by
Rick Reynolds

To
Beth

From
Melanie

B

BERKLEY BOOKS, NEW YORK

CAT NIPS!

feline cuisine

**A Berkley Book / published by arrangement with
Wieser & Wieser, Inc.**

PRINTING HISTORY
Berkley trade paperback edition / November 1992

Book design and mechanicals by
Media Dynamics
Armonk, New York 10504

ISBN: 0-425-13512-8

A BERKLEY BOOK ® TM 757,375

Berkley Books are published by
The Berkley Publishing Group,
200 Madison Avenue, New York, New York 10016.
The name **"BERKLEY"** and the **"B"** logo
are trademarks belonging to Berkley Publishing Corporation.

PRINTED IN THE UNITED STATES OF AMERICA

10   9   8   7   6   5   4   3   2   1

Contents

Cat Nips!

1 THE WAY TO A CAT'S

A Foreword

Our cat Syd loves to play and eat and sleep in endless combinations. He tries to include us in all his activities and in return we offer him a special selection of foods that add variety and nutrition to his diet. No one has ever proven that cats need variety and Syd would argue that no one has ever proven that people need variety. In our house though, "variety is the spice of life" and that's what this book is about.

It is no wonder that we humans are interested in menu variety. With our privileged position at the head of the food chain, we have a lot of choice in what we eat. Those animals below us on the food chain arguably spend more time looking over their shoulders to see who's gaining on them than they do thinking about cuisine. So we assume that food variety is a privilege of our position at the top of the hierarchy.

It wasn't always this way. When the saber-toothed tigers roamed the earth, humans and cats probably took turns having each other for dinner. Even today, there are parts of the world where the great cats, like the tiger and the lion, the jaguar and the cheetah, the cougar and the puma, the lynx and our own Syd all

HEART

hunt with near impunity. In the distant future, there's no saying what species may be on top of the food chain, so we should be nice to our pets, just in case.

Most animals – humans included – can exist on a monotonous diet. Our children are evidence of that. Since our cats can't be interviewed, we conveniently conclude that routine is something they desire. It is a human prejudice to think that we are the only warm-blooded species capable of appreciating the five senses, that only our experiences are relevant.

Cats have a sense of smell four times as great as our own. The feline nose is highly sensitive to the nitrogen compounds given off by spoiled food, allowing cats to evaluate freshness. In addition, cats have organs on the roofs of their mouths that are capable of analyzing both smell and taste simultaneously.

Perhaps most amazing, our cats can smell minute changes in our skin chemistry caused by illness, anger or grief. In reaction, they may try to comfort us, get angry or suffer panic attacks. Even when we mask our natural body odors with perfumes and deodorants, we cannot throw our cats off the scent of our emotions. Cats can tell when there's "something in the air," usually long before we ourselves know. What many consider to be the cat's sixth sense may very well be their sense of smell. In comparison, we must be missing the world's most subtle smells.

It is impossible to document with any precision how our feline friends perceive flavor. The line between "mandatory" and "recreational" eating is blurred since we can't chat with our cats about their dining experiences. In general our cats tend to be more connoisseurs than gluttons. Designed to eat meat, cats have many fewer "sweet" receptors than, for instance, dogs, and until recently it was thought that they had none at all. Our friend Pat had a cat who would walk across hot coals to get her ration of cantaloupe. Other cats have a fondness for orange slices or raisins, suggesting that some sweet signal must be getting through to the brain. By and large though, cats prefer meats and seafood, grains and vegetables. Variety is important for a nutritionally balanced diet.

Not all cats are finicky eaters, as evidenced by our cat Syd. As my cousin Jared would say, "Food is his favorite dish." Syd will sample a smorgasbord, savoring every morsel as if it were his last. Between swallows, he squints his eyes and contemplates how great life is. During long eating sessions, friends have remarked that Syd's stripes get noticeably farther apart.

The sense of hearing is also far more advanced in cats than in people. They can pick up sounds two octaves higher than we can, and can hear better than even dogs. When a small, far-off rodent emits an all but imperceptible squeak, Syd's ears rotate like twin satellite tracking dishes, each independently guided by fifteen muscles, stretching and contracting to locate its source. My human friend Bud, to everyone's amazement, can wiggle both of his ears separately and does so at parties. But Bud can't find his dinner with them.

Even while sleeping, Syd's ears and mind are alive, searching the airwaves for signs of life in the near universe. Able to track two sounds with five degrees of separation and one tenth of a note in difference, cats continuously monitor a world teeming with life to which we humans are all but oblivious. In her book *Secrets of the Cat*, Barbara Holland quips about her blue-eyed cat named Barney who can ". . . hear the difference between milk and water being poured into a bowl . . . can hear paint drying, grass growing, hair turning gray [and] time passing." Hear! Hear!

While cats' eyes are very similar to ours, they can see things we cannot. Mirrors in back of their eyes gather infinitesimal remnants of light and amplify them to useable levels. Our furry little companions can see with eighty percent less light than we require, giving them remarkable night vision. Their total view is wider than ours by seventy-five degrees and their binocular vision is wider by ten degrees, an adaptation especially suited to hunting.

The cat's eye is not only a formidable seeing machine, but an image of beauty and mystery, as well. Looking into a cat's eyes is like taking a journey into the unknowable. As close as we are, they are not us.

To some extent, cats can interpret visual symbols and translate them into the real world. For example, Syd "watches" TV. When we put the set down on the floor, he will swat at the birds, the cars and even the World Federation wrestlers who go flying across the screen. He knows it's fake. To Syd, TV is like a giant video game. Generally, he likes the less sophisticated action shows, like the kind his father watches.

I am convinced that cats are especially suited to enjoy their senses. When Syd enters the room, he will gradually gravitate toward one of us. Eventually, he will brush against us to express his connection, his ownership. When his head is scratched, his purring diesels up your arm and tickles your sense of well-being. Our cat friends clearly live in the realm of the senses.

When we humans begin to lose our bias, we realize that the world was not made exclusively for us. Through the use of tools, we have extended our abilities and have changed the landscape, in some places beyond recognition. Cats have never needed tools. Their bodies routinely perform unbelievable feats with such grace, they disguise all mechanical function. Their undulating, fluid motion all but denies the physical structures that lie beneath. While birds and fish travel through fluid mediums, they conform to the flow. Cats flow through a rigid world, transforming it into a more useful and beautiful state. They move in a stream of their own making, like pure energy. Out of respect, gravity seems to loosen its grip to allow these splendid creatures to pass.

With their almost supernatural qualities, it is no wonder that cats have been worshipped (and, tragically, vilified) throughout recorded history. What they do simply cannot be done better. To be blind to the miracle of the cat is to miss their unique place in the animal kingdom. For all our human ingenuity, I wonder if we will ever learn to blend as harmoniously into our surroundings as our cats do.

Ralph Waldo Emerson once proclaimed that "Beauty is its own excuse for being." The cat is pure beauty. With their poetic curves, their physical grace and their capacity for contentment, our cats show us the beauty of being.

The way to a cat's heart then is through his senses, not just through his stomach. This book is about cooking for your cat and about nurturing your relationship. It is about interacting with another species and, in the process, discovering something nice about your own.

2 IN THE BELLY OF THE

An Introduction to the Recipes

"I shall never forget the indulgence with which Dr. Johnson treated Hodge, his cat, for whom he himself used to go out and buy oysters, lest the servants, having that trouble, should take a dislike to the poor creature."

— James Boswell on the 18th-century English poet Samuel Johnson

Shakespeare once proclaimed, "The world's mine oyster." While it was never clear to me exactly what that meant, our cat Syd knows, at least in the literal sense. In addition to loving oysters, Syd has the attitude that the world was created for him and that he is worthy of the best.

"All cats are possessed of a proud spirit, and the surest way to forfeit the esteem of a cat is to treat him as an inferior being."

— Michael Joseph

Fortunately for Syd, he was adopted by a seafood-loving family.

To understand our cats' eating habits, we must understand the nature of their prey. In the wild, cats dine on small rodents, birds and fish. As you can imagine, the meat on an ordinary mouse doesn't amount to much, even by cat standards. Since their meals tend to come in tiny packages, cats prefer to eat frequently, consuming one mouse's worth of food per meal. Like their wild relatives, the domestic cat may consume 10-20 small meals over

BEAST

the course of a day, digesting each one before starting the next.

Having frequent little meals has its advantages. Cats are predators, not scavengers. They like freshly killed prey and are exquisitely suited to smelling the difference between new and old food. In fact, the cat's sense of smell is probably its most important sense when it comes to selecting food.

The question then becomes: How can we accommodate the natural feeding patterns cats experience in the field within the constraints of our hectic schedules? The average portion we feed our cats is equivalent to five mice, so it is not surprising our cats refuse most of what they are offered. As they come back for their subsequent feedings, the food gets progressively less appetizing as its freshness deteriorates. In addition, refrigerated food is so much colder than the ideal 86 degrees Fahrenheit of freshly killed prey (cats' tongues are also 86 degrees F), that many cats will refuse their food for that reason alone.

Obviously it is not possible to serve our feline friends ten or more freshly prepared meals, each at 86 degrees Fahrenheit. To some extent, our cats, like us, must conform to the fast food mentality of our times, eating commercially produced food in less than ideal portions. However, there are times when, like Samuel Johnson with his cat Hodge, we can indulge our pets with a specially prepared treat that plays to their natural tastes and sensitivities.

There are those of you out there who are skeptical about your cat's desire for a varied menu. Raise your hands. It is true that cats fed a monotonous diet over long periods of time will eventually lose interest in trying new foods, regardless of how inviting they are. To some extent, we humans unknowingly promote this "neophobia," or fear of the new, in our cats.

Wild cats have an inborn "food variety mechanism" that ensures they do not become overly dependent on one kind of prey. From time to time, their usual food source, though plentiful, will become unattractive and the cat will switch. With domestic cats that have  been fed the same diet day in and day out, their "food variety mechanism" degrades and eventually disappears altogether. New foods and smells become threatening to these cats. Interestingly, the same phenomenon also works in reverse. Cats who are accustomed to great variety may occasionally refuse to eat old favorites.

In general, eating a variety of foods is good for both cats and humans alike. It should be remembered, however, that as pure carnivores cats, unlike people, must have meat products in their diets to survive. Animal proteins provide cats with taurine, an amino acid essential to eyesight; animal fats are vital to the manufacture of fatty acids; and, the liver, kidney, and fish oils provide the cat's only source of vitamin A. While the human body can manufacture these substances from plants, cats cannot. That is not to say that cats shouldn't have fruits and vegetables. In the wild they get sufficient plant matter from the contents of the prey animal's stomach, and it is necessary for a balanced diet.

Syd's main meal consists of a high quality, commercially produced cat food that supplies his daily nutritional requirement. Cat owners are demanding higher standards and the results are encouraging. There are stricter federal standards, with more natural and nutritious ingredients and varieties designed to meet the special needs of kittens, older cats, cats with allergies and more. It's up to you to read the labels carefully and choose the brand that best satisfies your standards and your cat's nutritional needs.

While the recipes that follow are filled with natural, wholesome ingredients, they are meant to supplement the regular diet, not replace it. These treats have been tested by Syd and our other feline consultants and were enthusiastically received. But cats, like people, have different taste preferences and varying abilities to digest certain foods. So the first time you try any new food on your cat, keep the portion small and see what happens.

Finally, why make homemade treats for your cat? Why spend the afternoon turning ground-up mackerel into delicacies that could only appeal to our feline friends? Why go hunting for catnip, fish oil and bone meal, when the market is already stocked to the rafters with ready-to-eat goodies? Will your cat be healthier . . . happier? Will his life be richer? We think so. But there is another benefit to cooking for your pet. It is a way to connect with your cat and a time to focus on your special relationship.

3 FROM SCRATCH

Our Feline Consultants and Their Recipes

SYD

SYD

Chappaqua, New York

> **"Drowsing, they take the noble attitude
> of a great sphinx, who, in a desert land,
> Sleeps always, dreaming dreams that
> have no end."**
> — **Charles Baudelaire**

Most cats nap for up to eighteen hours a day. For our Syd, there are not enough hours in the day for rest. Syd's lack of ambition is legendary, even among cats. He simply refuses to earn an honest dollar, preferring instead to flaunt his lifestyle as a living repudiation of the Puritan work ethic; a contemplative connoisseur of comfort. Many people tire just watching him.

An Orange Tabby, Syd wandered in from the farm fields surrounding our family retreat in Maine, sampled the food and decided to stay. Not fat, he is a cat of immense proportions with pronounced stripes and, as far as anyone can tell, considerable intelligence.

Syd correctly concluded early on that hunting was not his sport. He could not accelerate, decelerate or change directions like animals of normal weight. But even if he could, Syd wouldn't. The food is simply too good at home to bother messing about with lesser creatures.

Instead, when Syd finds himself awake, he will stroll off like a sumo wrestler in search of the odd tom with whom he can have a scuffle. Then he returns home for a meal and a snooze.

Syd's Couch Potato Fritters with Anchovies . . .

SYD'S COUCH POTATO FRITTERS WITH ANCHOVIES

Next time you're baking potatoes, throw an extra one in for your cat!

1 potato, baked
1 tablespoon cottage cheese
4 canned anchovies, chopped
1 egg, beaten
Vegetable oil, as needed

Peel the potatoe and mash it with the cottage cheese. Mix in the anchovies and the egg. Lightly grease a non-stick skillet and heat over a medium flame. Drop ½ teaspoonfuls of the mixture onto skillet and fry for about 4 minutes per side. The fritters will be puffy and golden brown. Allow fritters to cool on paper towels. Store in an airtight container in the refrigerator.

MINNIE

MINNIE

Englewood, New Jersey

Minnie's life is nicely organized. Four times a day, just as she has done for the last fifteen years, Minnie goes to the kitchen door and stretches high to reach a little cowbell hanging from the doorknob. When the bell tinkles, it means Minnie needs to do the same.

Once outdoors, Minnie takes care of business and afterward she hides behind a bush to lie in wait for her canine-sister, Daisy, to happen along. Then, after ambushing the poor dog for the millionth time, Minnie heads for the backyard, climbs thirty feet up a pine tree, tightropes out along a branch and enters her house through a specially designed third-story window. Once inside she naps on her mom's pillow until a little bell goes off in her head and she sets out once again for the kitchen door.

Minnie has several diversions to break up the routine. One activity she looks forward to is "Broom Grooming." Every time her parents attempt to sweep the floors, Minnie flattens out spread-eagle like a tiger rug and begs to be broomed. On slippery floors, Minnie is pushed along like a giant, living dust mop. The pleasure she gets from this is hard to translate into human terms, but for those few precious moments, Minnie is swept away into a better world.

The following recipe is formulated especially for older cats and, though low in calories, it will sweep your fussy feline off her feet.

Minnie's Morsels for Mature Cats . . .

Cat Nips!

MINNIE'S MORSELS
FOR MATURE CATS

"Immature" cats will also love these treats. Serve them at room temperature.

1 can sardines, packed in olive oil
1 cup whole grain bread crumbs
1 egg, beaten
1/2 teaspoon brewer's yeast, optional

Preheat oven to 325 degrees

Pour entire contents of sardine can into
a medium-sized bowl. Using a fork, mash
the sardines into tiny pieces. Add the
remaining ingredients and mix well.
Drop 1/4 teaspoonfuls of the mixture
onto a lightly greased cookie sheet.
Bake for 7 minutes. Cool and store in
an airtight container in the refrigerator.

FOG

FOG

San Francisco, California

Near the ocean in the Sunset district of San Francisco lives a feline named Fog. A Brown Mackerel Norwegian Forest cat, Fog's lines are blurred by her double coat of thick underfur and long outer guard hairs. This soft-edged "Wegie" keeps house in her basement apartment while her dad, a traveling salesman, is on the road.

Being alone much of the time, Fog learned how to open doors by lifting latches and could even get herself a drink by turning faucets on and scooping water up to her mouth with her paw. One trick Fog never learned was turning the faucets off. On some months her dad's water bill was so high he was getting calls from swimming pool cleaning services.

During one two-day stretch when Fog's dad was away, a problem developed in one of the bathroom drains and when the cat turned on the water a flood of biblical proportions resulted. By the time the good salesman made it home, his furniture had formed a flotilla and his wonderful Fog was nowhere to be seen. Tears welled up in his eyes as he sloshed from room to room through the shin-deep water, screaming his cat's name. As he neared his breaking point,

Fog emerged from a closet drifting on a piece of flotsam. She meowed sheepishly and jumped over to her father. With his cat in his arms, Fog's dad sat down in the water . . . and wept.

Since he quit his job to be closer to his cat, Fog's dad has plenty of time to make her favorite dish.

Fog's Seafood Fajitas . . .

FOG'S SEAFOOD FAJITAS

Fog prefers her fajitas with salmon, though other fillings can be substituted to satisfy your cat's cravings.

¹/₄ cup cooked salmon (remove any bones)
1 teaspoon mayonnaise
¹/₂ teaspoon finely chopped chives
2 flour tortillas
¹/₄ cup grated Monterey Jack cheese

Mash the salmon with the mayonnaise and mix in the chives. Spread one of the tortillas evenly with the salmon mixture. Sprinkle the cheese over the salmon and top with the remaining tortilla. Press the tortillas together. Heat a large non-stick skillet until quite hot. Place the tortillas in the skillet, cheese side down. Cook for about 3 minutes until the cheese is melted. Flip the tortillas over and continue to cook the other side for another minute. Remove to a plate and allow to cool before cutting into ¹/₂." squares (or use tiny cookie cutters, if you have them). Serve these at room temperature and store in the refrigerator.

ROACH

ROACH

Hatfield, Massachusetts

According to her mother, Roach is a one man cat – a cat who has never come to terms with the fact that her tom, a human named Tom, is married to her mother. In bed Roach, an Exotic Shorthair, sleeps between her parents, careful not to allow any human-to-human contact. If by accident Roach's mom should brush against her legal husband, the cat will gently bite the offending protrusion. If it happens again, all hell breaks loose.

Roach's dad doesn't recognize the problem and regards the cat as a loyal and affectionate friend. Except for once offering to buy a second bed, he has refused to talk about the subject altogether.

Instead, he spends his free time playing Roach's favorite game, "Cat Fishing," in which he expertly casts a cloth mouse down the hall and into the dining room using a fly rod and three-pound test line. Then, from his fighting chair, he skillfully plays out line and reels it back in, cautious not to allow any slack to form. At the end of the struggle, Roach emerges mouse in mouth and they both squeal with delight.

Roach's mom, desperate for an audience with her husband, devised this recipe to lure her cat away from him.

Roach's Distraction Dinner . . .

Cat Nips!

ROACH'S DISTRACTION DINNER

This casserole makes a special meal for your cat. Roach eats about six ounces at a time. The rest is frozen in six-ounce portions for later use.

1 slice bacon
10 ounces ground turkey
2 cups cooked elbow macaroni
$\frac{1}{3}$ cup peas, fresh or frozen
$\frac{1}{3}$ cup water or chicken stock
$\frac{1}{4}$ cup V-8 juice

Cut the bacon into $\frac{1}{4}$" pieces and fry them in a large skillet, over medium heat, until thoroughly cooked. Add the turkey and cook, stirring often, until meat has lost its pink color. Add the remaining ingredients and cook for about 10 minutes. Allow to cool to room temperature before serving.

CLINT

CLINT

Harriman, New York

"Ignorant people think it's the noise which fighting cats make that's so aggravating, but it ain't so; it's the sickening grammar they use."
— Mark Twain

This bruiser of a cat plays hard, fights hard, eats hard and talks tough! As a kitten, Clint would get into shouting matches with his stepbrother and, although he was declawed, he was still tough as nails. Appropriately, this scrappy cat was named after Clint Eastwood.

Clint's belligerence is no surprise to those who witnessed his personal cataclysm. Before he was three months old, Clint was rescued from a burning apartment by a firefighter who braved the flames to reach the kitten. Near death, Clint was thrown from a shattered window, falling five stories before being caught in a blanket by a cheering crowd. When Clint's dad arrived on the scene, his vociferous white tabby with orange patches was jet black and blowing smoke. Both man and beast knew at that moment how special their relationship was.

Clint is verbal to the point of annoyance. He simply talks too much. And in spite of his large vocabulary, Clint chooses to utter vulgarities, having learned early on that they get the most attention and make the best bluffs.

By the end of the day, this clamorous kitty has worked up an appetite for his favorite food, scungelli salad. Being the tough cat that he is, Clint does not chew the octopus, preferring instead to swallow it whole. **Clint's Octopussy Salad . . .**

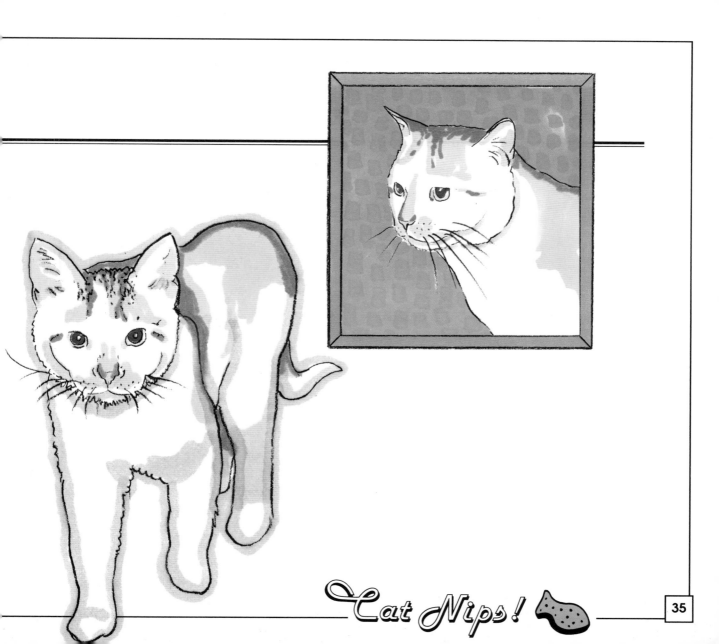

Cat Nips!

CLINT'S OCTOPUSSY SALAD

This salad tastes so good, you may find yourself bullying your cat to give you some!

½ pound octopus
1 tablespoon olive oil
1 teaspoon lemon juice
1 tablespoon finely chopped red pepper
1 tablespoon finely chopped celery
1 teaspoon chopped chives
¼ teaspoon catnip, optional

Put the octopus in a medium saucepan and cover with cold water. Bring the water to a boil and cook the octopus just until the meat feels firm. This will only take a few minutes. Remove the octopus from the water and when cool enough to touch, chop it into tiny pieces. Combine with the remaining ingredients and toss.

ELLA

Cat Nips!

ELLA

Seekonk, Massachusetts

Ella makes a great-looking owl. A Tortoiseshell Persian with large, round, forward-facing eyes, a tucked-in face and tufted ears, she resembles the North American Hoot Owl. From a distance, only her long fluffy tail betrays the fact that this owl is a cat.

With a face only a mouse could hate, Ella's permanent pucker is cute beyond words. Small for a Tortie, Ella is sixteen pounds lighter than her stepbrother, Mr. Floyd. Though she lacks his size, she has the presence of an elephant in a one-car garage. Ella achieves this by nesting in a slightly undersized Japanese Oribe bowl – a living still life atop the dining table.

From this throne, Ella can monitor all of the activity in the apartment. And, it is here she huddles, living completely on her own terms, complaining from time to time about absolutely nothing, just to let you know that life is not a bowl of cherries.

This impressive creature happens to share our passion for Häagen–Dazs frozen yogurt. While many Persians are lactose intolerant, Ella is only intolerant of those who think she is. For the purpose of this book, however, we will focus on Ella's more healthful appreciation of Japanese art and cuisine.

Ella's Sumptuous Sushi Rolls . . .

ELLA'S SUMPTUOUS SUSHI ROLLS

Next time you make lasagna, save a couple noodles for this recipe. You can vary the filling to satisfy your kitty's craving. Your cat will think these look as good as they taste.

2 cooked lasagna noodles
¼ cup cooked salmon or other boneless fish
¼ cup alfalfa sprouts
Flaked norie (edible seaweed), optional

Lay noodles out on waxed paper. Cut each noodle in half lengthwise. In a small bowl mash the salmon into tiny pieces. Spread a thin layer of salmon on each noodle leaving about ½" uncovered at each end. Sprinkle each noodle with alfalfa sprouts and some norie. Beginning at one end, roll each noodle pinwheel style, as tightly as possible. Cut the rolls into ¼" slices and serve. Store tightly wrapped in the refrigerator.

MIKEY

MIKEY

New York, New York

S ome toms dream of beguiling Burmese beauties, multitudes of mice and cartloads of catnip. Not Mikey. What gets Mikey's attention is that tropical fruit in a hostile package the pineapple.

Mikey, a sealpoint Siamese, worships, caresses and guards his prickly, spiny-leafed object of desire. To accommodate this fetish, his mother bought a stand of wire hearts to hold Mikey's pineapple upright, in a more animated position.

In the evening, when the fruit is put to bed in the refrigerator, Mikey stages an all-night vigil at the foot of the door, moaning and whining until morning when they are again reunited.

On one occasion, when Mikey's pineapple met an untimely end at the hands of an unknowing house guest, the cat actually knocked over the garbage in a fruitless effort to rescue his decapitated love. Days later he was still pining over it.

Even pineapples who escape the knife eventually wither, so Mikey's parents must go out periodically in search of a fresh fruit that resembles his last. Fortunately, love being fickle, Mikey apparently doesn't notice the switch.

Since you cannot have your pineapple and eat it too, Mikey's recipe does not contain the "P" word.

Mikey's Mackerel Munchie . . .

Cat Nips!

MIKEY'S MACKEREL MUNCHIE

Mikey thinks these are good and fishy. Just the way he likes his treats!

½ cup canned mackerel, drained
1 cup whole grain bread crumbs
1 tablespoon vegetable oil
1 egg, beaten
½ teaspoon brewer's yeast, optional

Preheat the oven to 350 degrees.

In a medium-sized bowl, mash the mackerel with a fork into tiny pieces. Combine it with the remaining ingredients and mix them well. Drop the mixture by ¼ teaspoonfuls onto a greased cookie sheet. Bake for 8 minutes. Cool to room temperature and store in an airtight container in the refrigerator.

HOCUS POCUS

Cat Nips!

HOCUS POCUS

Quincy, Massachusetts

Before Hocus Pocus's mother went abroad, she dropped the cat off at her dad's place, along with a note listing her special instructions. In addition to his regular food, the cat would require eye drops twice a day and one sinkful of water three times a day with meals.

Now, why would an eight-pound Himalayan need three sinkfuls of water per day? The gardener doesn't even use that much! The note went on to explain that Hocus would only drink from a sink filled to the brim with freshly drawn water. Naturally, Hocus's grandfather ignored this ridiculous example of animal indulgence.

Soon, the cat began to dry out. Rejecting the water in his bowl, Hocus would jump up on the kitchen counter and circle the sink, meowing in a pathetic, raspy little voice. After several days, there was no getting around it. The puss was parched.

Fearful of losing his daughter's affection, Granddad filled the sink to the gunwales. Hocus then gracefully leaned over the basin, took several licks and wandered off for a nap.

Three times a day now, like clockwork, Granddad fills up the kitchen sink so that Hocus can properly moisten his gums. With life back in order, the two wait for Mom's return.

These juicy hors d'oeuvres were specially created for Hocus to wet his whistle while whetting his appetite.

Hocus Pocus's Magically Moist Morsels . . .

HOCUS POCUS'S MAGICALLY MOIST MORSELS

Most cats find these little meatballs irresistible. Ground turkey works just as well as the ground beef. Adjust the size of the meatballs according to the size of your cat. We serve these to our cat at room temperature or slightly warmed in the microwave.

½ pound ground beef
1 small carrot, finely grated
1 tablespoon grated cheese
1 teaspoon brewer's yeast
1 teaspoon dried catnip
½ cup whole wheat bread crumbs
1 egg, beaten
1 tablespoon tomato paste

Preheat the oven to 350 degrees.

In a medium-sized bowl, combine the ground beef, carrot, cheese, brewer's yeast, catnip and bread crumbs. Add the egg and tomato paste and mix well.

Using your hands, roll the mixture into walnut-sized meatballs and place on a lightly greased cookie sheet. Bake for about 15 minutes until the meatballs are brown and firm. Cool the meatballs completely before storing in an airtight container in the refrigerator. These freeze well. This makes about 2 dozen.

WILTON

WILTON

New York, New York

Most cats play with string. Willie plays the strings.

It all started when this hip downtown black and white cat began sniffing out rubber bands at his Manhattan pad. Willie could track down a rubber band anywhere. On bouquets of flowers, on newspapers, or even around letters in a desk drawer, Willie would find a rubber band and when he did, he'd pluck it. All day long the "plink, plink, plink" of Willie's plucking could be heard around the flat. After several dozen "plinks," the rubber band would snap and Willie would look for another.

Finally it dawned on Willie's mom that this cool cat might be musically inclined. Without delay, she went out and bought him a cheap plastic guitar and, in short order, Willie was not only plucking on it, but strumming as well. With Willie's built-in finger picks, the notes came out crisp and clean, and though the tunes were repetitive, "they were no more monotonous than most new age music."

The landlord didn't agree and moved to have the guitar evicted.

Now, Willie is back to plucking rubber bands, his budding career ending on a sour note.

Unbelievable as it may seem, Willie's mother says her plucky little musician loves string beans and beets. You can't make this stuff up.

Willie's String Bean and Beet Medley . . .

Cat Nips!

WILLIE'S STRING BEAN AND BEET MEDLEY

Not all cats will share Willie's love for string beans and beets. However, many cats do seem to enjoy vegetables which may explain their attraction to house plants. Try experimenting with small amounts of other vegetables, such as finely grated carrots or zucchini or alfalfa sprouts.

3 cooked string beans
1 small cooked beet
¹/₂ teaspoon olive oil
1 tablespoon vegetable & beef baby food
catnip

Thinly slice the string beans. Chop or grate the beet. In a small bowl, mix the olive oil with the baby food. Add the vegetables and toss. Sprinkle with catnip and serve.

BONNIE

Cat Nips!

BONNIE

Henrietta, New York

An old college friend of ours had a cat named Bonnie who worshipped the ground he walked on. In fact, Bonnie worshipped the shoes that touched the ground that he walked on. When her dad was away Bonnie slept in his clothes closet, nestled among the wing tips, Hush Puppies and sneakers. The smells in there were nice and familiar and occasionally there would be an old ripe sock to chew on.

Bonnie loved to make ball-ups out of the cellophane and foil she recycled from her dad's cigarette packs. After rolling up several such balls, she'd run straight for the closet and insert them, like little calling cards, deep into the toes of her dad's shoes. Every morning, in a kind of shell game, Bonnie's dad was faced with a dozen shoes, only a few of which contained ball-ups. Since it was not practical to shake out all of the shoes, all of the time, Bonnie's dad simply slipped a pair on, and if a shoe felt too small, he'd empty it. It was manageable.

The problem came when Bonnie's dad quit smoking. With her raw materials cut off, Bonnie could no longer communicate. She became sullen and wouldn't eat. Her dad grew more and more worried and even considered taking up smoking again.

Finally, in a flash of brilliance, Bonnie's dad cut up little strips of aluminum foil and left them around the house. In short order, Bonnie's little gestures of love began showing up in her dad's shoes again, and all was right with the world.

Bonnie's Shoestring Potatoes with Sole . . .

BONNIE'S SHOESTRING POTATOES WITH SOLE

Any kind of leftover fish will work well in this recipe. Just be sure to carefully remove any bones!

½ to 1 cup cooked, boneless sole
1 potato, grated
1 egg, beaten
1 teaspoon chopped chives, optional
vegetable oil, as needed

Mash the fish into tiny pieces. Put the grated potato into a strainer and press out as much moisture as possible. Combine all the ingredients except the oil and mix well. Lightly oil a large nonstick skillet and heat over a medium flame until quite hot. Drop ¼ teaspoonfuls of the mixture into the skillet and gently flatten with a spatula. Cook for about 5 minutes on each side. The little fritters should be golden brown and cooked through. When they're done, cool them on paper towels. Store in an airtight container in the refrigerator.

CIELITO LINDO

CIELITO LINDO

Saint Remy, New York

Cielito Lindo used to be quite unpleasant. Though named after the Mexican term for "my little sweet one," Señorita Cielito was anything but. This mostly black, part Burmese cat would swat and hiss at all who approached her.

Her stepbrother, Lorenzo, was by contrast a big loveable Maine Coon Cat ". . . who would jump up, flip upside down and park in your lap with his engine idling." The two cats could not have been more different.

One day Lorenzo mysteriously vanished. With all the windows and doors locked tight and no sign of a break-in, Lorenzo's disappearance was as confusing as it was sad. Suddenly, Cielito began to take on Lorenzo's agreeable personality. The neighbors, skeptical of her metamorphosis, suspected that Cielito had a hand in Lorenzo's demise. One even suggested weighing her.

Today, only Cielito knows what happened to poor Lorenzo, and the cat's got her tongue. She spends her days patrolling the catwalks of her country estate, "Casa de Campo," and has managed to keep her dark secret and pleasing disposition intact.

Cielito's love of cantaloupe, however, has been no secret and even the subtle sound of a knife slicing through this marvelous melon is enough to send her running from the far corners of the house.

Cielito's Cantaloupe Cocktail . . .

Cat Nips!

CIELITO'S CANTALOUPE COCKTAIL

Cielito thinks this recipe is the cat's meow! It seems that she's no exception. Most cats go crazy over cantaloupe.

½ cup fresh, ripe cantaloupe,
*   cut into small chunks*
¼ cup plain yogurt
½ teaspoon honey, optional
catnip

Combine the cantaloupe with the yogurt. Drizzle the honey on top, if desired, and sprinkle with catnip. You may feel like making one of these cocktails for yourself! Just leave off the catnip.

BINGO

BINGO

B ingo is a born collaborator. He works with his mom, a composer and pianist who teamed up with the cat to break the solitude artists often feel in their lonely quest for perfection. Bingo snores under the piano bench while his mom pounds out the musical passages that comprise her livelihood. Whenever the good composer hits a lousy note... "Bingo abruptly wakes up and changes his position, indicating that more work needs to be done on that measure." When the composition is going smoothly, Bingo sleeps.

One day, Bingo's mom decided that two cats would be twice as helpful as one, so she went out and bought her cat a brother. That struck a bad chord with Bingo. He was livid. To express his displeasure, Bingo jumped up on his mom's piano and shredded her sheet music. Then he stomped up and down the keyboard in a vitriolic dance of fragmented chords and violent tempo changes.

To make matters worse, Bingo's new brother wailed every time his mother played a major seventh chord. Soon, it was all too evident that a commiserating cat was far preferable to a kitty who accompanied, so the new arrival was given to the composer's sister.

Now, Bingo is back under the piano bench making music with his mother.

Bingo's Clams Allegro . . .

BINGO'S CLAMS ALLEGRO

Some cats, like Bingo, have sophisticated tastes in food. In addition to this dish, Bingo enjoys shrimp curry and stir fry beef and vegetables. Variety is beneficial to the cat.

1 small clove garlic, chopped
1 tablespoon olive oil
1 can chopped clams, undrained
1 teaspoon chopped parsley
1 cup cooked egg pastina (tiny pasta)
1 tablespoon grated Parmesan or
   Romano cheese

In a medium-sized skillet, cook the garlic in the olive oil for five minutes. Add the clams, the parsley and the pasta. Cook for five minutes, and toss in the cheese. Cool and serve at room temperature. Store the leftovers, tightly covered in the refrigerator.

TIGGER

TIGGER

Turner, Maine

A predator, Tigger is not. He and his two brothers were hired on fourteen years ago to help control the rodent population on his parents' apple farm. Soon it was apparent that one of the three mouseketeers was a fraud.

Tigger's brothers would routinely catch small vermin and deposit their remains at the foot of the kitchen door for inspection. Tigger preferred stalking the old rusty cans and plastic six-pack fasteners he found in the orchards. More often than not, Tigger would end up being caught by his catch, only to return home wearing it. It was a sore topic around the farm for over a dozen years.

Then one afternoon, Tigger appeared at the kitchen door looking uncharacteristically pleased with himself. Around his mid-section was a rusted wire hoop and in his mouth was a large ripe tomato stolen from the neighboring farm. Proudly, Tigger placed his plump red trophy next to his bothers' catch for the day. There, shoulder to shoulder with several unfortunate rodents, lay Tigger's tomato, showing no signs of a struggle except for four neat little fang holes.

We asked Tigger's father, point-blank, if he was disappointed waiting fourteen years only to have the cat bring home a tomato. "Hell no!" he replied. "We were hoping he'd go and get more!"

The point well taken, no one laughed.

Tigger's Tomato & Turkey Jerky . . .

Cat Nips!

TIGGER'S TOMATO & TURKEY JERKY

This chewy goodie is a great favorite with all the cats we know.

1 pound ground turkey
2 tablespoons tomato paste
½ teaspoon garlic powder
2 teaspoons brewer's yeast

Preheat oven to 120 degrees or the lowest setting.

Combine all the ingredients and mix well.

Line a jelly roll pan with foil and spread the meat mixture in it. Using your hands flatten the mixture to about ¼" thick. Place the meat in the oven and prop the oven door open a crack using a wooden spoon, so the moisture can escape. Bake for about 2 hours, until the meat is quite dry. Remove the meat from the oven and place another sheet foil over it. Grasping both sheets of foil, flip the meat over and peel the foil from the top. Place the meat back in the oven with the door propped open, and bake for another 1 to 2 hours. The meat will be red and dry, like jerky.

RED BUTTONS

Cat Nips!

RED BUTTONS

Fair Lawn, New Jersey

As handsome as he is, Red Buttons should not be in this book. He wags his tail when he's happy and chases it in circles when he's bored. He fetches, he grunts and snarls and gulps down two cans of food in one sitting. This confused carnivore even kicks out his hind legs after doing his business. No self-respecting feline would envy this dog trapped in a Red Persian's body.

What saves Red Buttons' identity is his catlike ability to entertain himself. For instance, when his mother is away at work, Red Buttons plays "Solitaire Catch" by running a paper ball up to the top of the stairs where he releases it, then beats it to the bottom, where he waits to catch it. He repeats this game for hours.

His hands-down favorite sport is "Flashlight Football," and even if his dad isn't home to play it, Red Buttons tackles the various sun spots that drift across the wall during the day.

At bedtime, when his parents are dog tired, Red Buttons nips at their heels to play one more game.

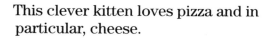

This clever kitten loves pizza and in particular, cheese.

Red Buttons' Cheesy Chewies . . .

RED BUTTONS' CHEESY CHEWIES

Many cats adore cheese and eggs, both of which are an excellent source of protein. If your cat is on the chubby side, leave out the bacon and use a lowfat cheese.

1 slice bacon, fried and crumbled
1 egg, beaten
½ cup grated cheese
½ cup cooked rice or bulgur
½ cup cooked vegetables, chopped,
grated or mashed (carrots, zucchini,
broccoli, etc.)
1 teaspoon brewer's yeast

Preheat oven to 350 degrees.

In a medium-sized bowl, combine all the ingredients and mix thoroughly. Drop by ½-teaspoonfuls onto a greased cookie sheet and bake for about 8 minutes. They should be set and lightly browned. Cool to room temperature and store in an airtight container in the refrigerator. These can also be frozen for longer storage.

EASBY

EASBY

LaGrangeville, New York

James "Easby" Smith is an aviator. On weekends this flying tiger takes off with his father, a private pilot, in their Mooney aircraft and together they make tracks in the sky. From his catbird seat, Easby is on top of the world watching the rodent-sized cars below and following the blinking lights of the various gauges. But Easby's love of flying once nearly killed him.

Easby and his dad used to live in a sixteenth-floor Manhattan penthouse. In the afternoons, Easby would walk up the fire escape to the roof where he would sun himself and pose for the office workers in the adjacent building. Soon, Easby began jumping from building to building, a span of several feet, in order to schmooze with his office friends across the way. It was on one of these leaps that Easby lost his footing and, to the horror of his fan club, fell sixteen stories to the pavement below.

The entire sixteenth-floor office emptied out and down to the street. Easby showed no signs of life. In a long, tearful procession they carried Easby's body up to his apartment. Easby's dad, upon seeing the cat, clutched him to his chest and ran the twelve blocks to the vet.

Easby was alive, but not by much. After doing all she could, the vet prescribed bed rest, lots of love and prayers. For a fortnight, Easby lay motionless in the center of his dad's bed. Dozens of visitors brought flowers and gifts each day. Then, after a month, James Easby Smith suddenly got up, stumbled over to his food dish and asked for his supper.

Miraculously, Easby is now back flying with his dad, pleased to be in the copilot's seat once again.

Easby's Miracle Prey . . .

Cat Nips!

EASBY'S MIRACLE PREY

This quick, easy recipe has all kinds of good stuff for your cat.

½ pound chicken livers, uncooked
1½ cups water
2 tablespoons V-8 juice
½ cup uncooked egg pastina (tiny pasta)
1 small carrot, grated

Place chicken livers in a medium-sized saucepan and cover with the water. Bring the water to a boil and simmer for about 7 minutes. Remove the chicken livers from the water and cool enough to chop into very small pieces. Add the remaining ingredients and chopped chicken livers to the cooking liquid and bring to a boil. Simmer for 5 minutes, stirring occasionally. Serve at room temperature.

SHOTSIE

SHOTSIE

Penn Yan, New York

The offspring of a champion Persian and an all-American alley cat, Shotsie has hints of greatness. If you look at her dead on, her magnificently flat and fluffy face totally eclipses the stripes and ticking of her humble body.

Shotsie is known in computer parlance, as a "hacker." She sits on her father's personal computer keyboard and follows the "flying toasters" that save the screen from "fluorescent burnout." No one knows what saves Shotsie from toaster burnout, but after two years she has shown no signs of boredom.

Occasionally, Shotsie will hit a command key that activates some of the peripheral equipment, and the bells and whistles that go off send her into a frenzy. Soon though, she is back on-line counting toasters.

Her dad figures that given enough time Shotsie could generate great material on the PC. But for now, he grabs the puss and boots up every morning – and off they go into computerland.

For Shotsie's recipe, we have included her favorite PC. Popcorn that is.

Shotsie's PC . . .

Cat Nips!

SHOTSIE'S PC

This is better than it sounds . . . at least your cat will think so!

1 tablespoon butter or margarine
1 teaspoon anchovy paste
2 cups popped popcorn
1 tablespoon grated Parmesan or Romano cheese
1 teaspoon brewer's yeast, optional

In a small pan, melt the butter or margarine and add the anchovy paste. Stir to mix thoroughly. Put the popcorn in a large bowl and toss it with the butter mixture. Your hands are the best tools for this job. Sprinkle the cheese and brewer's yeast over the popcorn and toss. Store in the refrigerator in an airtight container. Serve at room temperature.

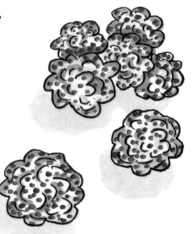

FRANCES THERESA

FRANCES THERESA

New York, New York

Champion Denimars Florence Mae, or Frances Theresa as she is known by her closest friends, is a startlingly beautiful white Scottish Fold. After an illustrious career on the show circuit, she retired from the stage in 1984 and now lives with her persnickety son, Monsignor Kelly and her agent/dad on Crosby Street in Soho.

Like all Scottish Folds, Frances Theresa descended from Suzy, a Scottish barn cat and a mutation of the British Shorthair. Scottish Folds look like cats in shower caps. Their ears are small and folded over in such a way as to make them disappear. In a pair of swim fins, "Folds" could pass for harp seals.

Frances Theresa was stone deaf from birth and consequently never learned to meow. Having a non-verbal mother, Monsignor Kelly long since gave up on conversation and spends most of his time in meditation or prayer. The resulting quiet can be disquieting to the uninitiated. Like tropical fish, the two cats float silently past one's peripheral vision, giving the apartment the feel of a giant aquarium. In fact, their father likens it to living underwater.

With some background bubble music playing on his CD player, Frances Theresa's dad sits back in his easy chair like an urban Jacques Cousteau and floats in his sea of cats.

Frances Theresa loves any kind of fowl, particularly chicken.

Frances Theresa's Chicken of the Sea . . .

Cat Nips!

FRANCES THERESA'S CHICKEN OF THE SEA

While protein is vital to a cat's survival, grains and vegetables are very beneficial too. This dish has it all!

2 cups water
½ cup uncooked brown rice
1 boneless chicken breast
½ cup chopped spinach
½ teaspoon kelp powder
catnip

Bring the water to a boil and add the rice. Reduce heat to low, cover and cook until the rice is fairly tender, about 25 minutes. Add the remaining ingredients and continue cooking, stirring occasionally, for 10 minutes or until the chicken breast is cooked through. Remove from heat. When the chicken is cool enough to handle, remove it from the pan and dice it into very small pieces. Add chicken pieces back into the stew and cool to room temperature. Before serving, garnish with a sprinkle of catnip. Store leftovers in the refrigerator or freezer.

HAVANA

Cat Nips!

HAVANA

Brooklyn, New York

Named for her elegant pedigree, Havana looks like a cross between a sealpoint Siamese and an expensive Cuban cigar. Part of a multicat family, Havana began rising through the hierarchy, like cream rising to the top. As a kitten, "Havana was the kind of child that grownups love and kids hate." She would fawn around her parents, but once they were out of sight she would beat up on her three Siamese sisters. Though she was the last cat to join the family, she soon ruled the roost.

One day when friends of Havana's parents came for a visit with their Chihuahua, Havana dropped what she was doing and took charge. As her mother described it, Havana and her sisters lined up perpendicularly to the Chihuahua, who was furiously wagging his tail to show his friendly intentions. Havana looked left and right along her flanks, took the cigarette butt out of her mouth, crushed it between her fingers, and advanced slowly toward the now trembling dog. As they backed the Chihuahua up against the down staircase, it looked for all the world like Havana and her sisters were going to force the poor little pooch to walk the plank.

Just at the moment the dog was about to lose it, Havana broke ranks, voiced something like "Be out of here by sundown!" and then strolled off to eat her dinner. One by one, her sisters followed until just one grateful creature remained.

Havana likes any fruit with appeal.

Havana's Banana Cakes . . .

HAVANA'S BANANA CAKES

Many cats enjoy an occasional nibble of fruit. Favorites seem to be grapes, cantaloupe, orange sections and even banana slices. Havana and her sisters love these little banana-flavored cakes.

½ cup whole wheat flour
¼ cup unbleached white flour
½ cup quick cooking rolled oats
¼ teaspoon baking soda
½ cup mashed ripe bananas (about 1 banana)
1 egg
1 tablespoon honey (optional)
1 tablespoon vegetable oil
¼ cup milk
½ teaspoon catnip

Preheat oven to 350 degrees.

Combine all the dry ingredients in a medium-sized bowl. In another bowl, beat together the bananas, egg, honey, oil and milk. Add to dry ingredients and mix well.

Drop ¼ teaspoonfuls of batter onto a greased cookie sheet. Bake for about 8 minutes, until firm. Cool completely and store in an airtight container in the refrigerator.

AUNT OLIVE'S
CATS

AUNT OLIVE'S CATS

Phoenix, Arizona

T hree cats and Aunt Olive got off the Greyhound bus in Phoenix after traveling for more than fifty hours. Their new home, a sprawling villa with twenty-three rooms, seemed to encapsulate the wide-open spaces Aunt Olive dreamed of when she lived in New York City. Not long after they settled in, three new cats joined the family, all strays that Aunt Olive took in, cleaned up and named. Every month brought several new orphans and, when the pride reached fifteen members, relatives back east started wondering where they would stay when they came for a visit. But Aunt Olive, a wealthy heiress, could do what she wanted, and what she wanted to do was nurture cats in need.

By the end of her first year in the southwest, the family grew to over twenty cats. The local veterinarian found Aunt Olive's charity enriching. He was doing a land-office business neutering her cats and giving them check-ups and shots. In fact, Aunt Olive was such a good customer, the vet started offering her free shuttle service to and from the clinic.

It wasn't long before the local officials got wind of

Aunt Olive's orphanage. Neighbors, worried about their property values, wanted the cathouse shut down. When health inspectors arrived at the front door, Aunt Olive nailed it shut. Warned that more officials armed with a court order were on their way, Aunt Olive calmly picked up the phone and called her vet. Within minutes, the driver from the animal hospital was at the back door service entrance loading cats, six at a time, into the van until eighteen cats were on their way to the clinic for an impromptu physical examination. Then Aunt Olive pulled the nails out of the front door and graciously received the health inspectors.

Inside, the scene was tranquil, with Aunt Olive knitting while several cats played with the ball of yarn. Following their exhaustive search of the house, the officials apologized for their intrusion, and to show that she harbored no hard feelings, Aunt Olive served them tea.

Aunt Olive's Kitty Vittles, for Twenty . . .

Cat Nips!

AUNT OLIVE'S KITTY VITTLES, FOR TWENTY

This recipe will make plenty of vittles for your cat and all your friends' cats. You can use these mackerel-flavored bits as individual treats or as a crunchy kibble to mix in with your cat's canned food.

3 cups whole wheat flour
2 cups soy flour
1 cup wheat germ
1 cup cornmeal
1 cup nonfat dry milk
1 tablespoon bone meal*
1 tablespoon kelp powder

½ cup brewer's yeast
1 (15 ounce) can mackerel
5 tablespoons vegetable oil
1 tablespoon cod liver oil
1 teaspoon garlic powder, optional
2 cups of water, or as needed

Preheat oven to 350 degrees.

Mix all the dry ingredients in a large bowl. In another bowl, mash the mackerel into small pieces. Mix in the oil and water. Add the mackerel mixture to the dry ingredients and mix thoroughly. The dough is tough, so use your hands.

Roll dough out to about ¼" thickness and cut into ¼" bits, using a knife or pizza wheel. Mound the bits onto greased cookie sheets and bake for 25 minutes. During baking, occasionally toss the bits with two wooden spoons, so they brown evenly. Turn the heat off and allow the treats to cool thoroughly before removing and storing in an airtight container in the refrigerator. This recipe freezes very well for longer storage.

*Bone meal can be purchased at healthfood stores or pet supply stores. Use only edible bone meal — not the garden variety.

4 PARTY ANIMAL

Special Treats for Special Occasions

Cats are great party animals. They're entertaining, mischievous and in the words of Gladys Taber, "Cats make exquisite photographs . . . they don't keep bouncing at you to be kissed just as you get the lense adjusted."

Birthdays, religious holidays like Christmas and Hanukkah, Valentine's Day and perhaps even Halloween are fine times to reflect on our feline relationships. There is nothing more perfect than gathering together with our cats, our children and in some cases our relatives for the purpose of connecting, cuddling and overeating. And when the party is over, you can count on the gratitude of your guest of honor.

> **"A cat can be trusted to purr when she is pleased,**
> **which is more than can be said for human beings."**
> **— William Ralph Inge,**
> **Rustic Moralist**

For those Scrooges out there who feel the cat unworthy of such consideration, take heed to the words of the 19th-century British writer George Elliot, who warned in her novel *Middlemarch*:

> **"Who can tell what criticisms**
> **Murr the cat may be passing on**
> **us beings of wider speculation?"**

The following are special recipes for unleashing our feelings on those special days.

KITTY CUSTARD AND KIBBLE

1 cup Aunt Olive's Kitty Vittles
²/₃ cup very hot milk
1 egg
1 egg yolk
1 tablespoon vegetable & beef baby food

Preheat the oven to 350 degrees.

Pour the hot milk over the Kitty Vittles and allow them to soak for about an hour, until the vittles are soft. Beat the egg, the egg yolk, and the baby food together. Combine the egg mixture with the Kitty Vittles mixture. Grease 4 small ramekins and fill each with equal amounts of the batter. Fill a baking dish with about an inch of hot water and place the ramekins in it. Bake for about 20 minutes, until set. Cool to room temperature before serving. Your cat may find the custard easier to eat if you spoon it onto a plate.

CATNIP CREPES
WITH HOLIDAYS' SAUCE

Catnip Crêpes

1 egg
¼ cup milk
⅓ cup flour
2 teaspoons vegetable oil
2 teaspoons dried catnip
¼ cup cottage cheese

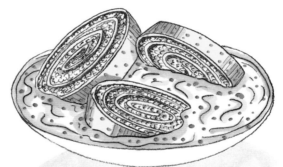

Combine all the ingredients, except the
cottage cheese, in a blender or food processor
and mix until the batter is frothy. Heat a large nonstick
skillet until moderately hot, then wipe very lightly with vegetable oil. Pour half the batter
into the hot skillet and quickly tilt the skillet around so the batter spreads evenly. Cook
crêpe for a few minutes until the edges lift easily from the pan. Flip and cook the second
side for about a minute. Remove to a plate and cook the second crêpe. Spread each crêpe
with a thin layer of cottage cheese and roll them up jelly roll style. Slice each roll into ½"
pieces. Serve crêpes with a dollop of "Holidays' Sauce" (recipe follows).

Holidays' Sauce

¼ cup heavy cream
½ teaspoon anchovy paste

In a small bowl whip cream until soft peaks form. Add the anchovy paste and beat for
another 20 seconds.

5 LAST LICKS

Some Final Thoughts

On the subject of the cat, Alan Devoe wrote:

"The things which a man gives him are not so precious or essential that he will trade them for his birthright, which is the right to be himself..."

By now you and your cat have shared your affection for one another. You've tasted what it's like to connect with a creature so different it could well have come from another planet, yet so familiar, it could be an extension of yourself. And in spite of the love you have lavished on your cat, he has remained as uncorrupted as any animal on earth.

In this age of confused values, where time equals money, we forget that it's time itself that's important. The time we share.

We close with this quote:

"God made the cat in order that man might have the pleasure of caressing the tiger."

— Ferand Méry